Steve Case
Internet Genius of America Online

INTERNET BIOGRAPHIES

BILL GATES
Software Genius of Microsoft
0-7660-1969-1

LARRY ELLISON
Database Genius of Oracle
0-7660-1974-8

ESTHER DYSON
Internet Visionary
0-7660-1973-X

STEVE CASE
Internet Genius of America Online
0-7660-1971-3

JEFF BEZOS
Business Genius of Amazon.com
0-7660-1972-1

STEVE JOBS
Computer Genius of Apple
0-7660-1970-5

INTERNET BIOGRAPHIES

Steve Case
Internet Genius of America Online

by Craig Peters

Enslow Publishers, Inc.
40 Industrial Road   PO Box 38
Box 398   Aldershot
Berkeley Heights, NJ 07922   Hants GU12 6BP
USA   UK
http://www.enslow.com

PRODUCED BY:
Chestnut Productions
Russell, Massachusetts

Editor and Picture Researcher: *Mary E. Hull*
Design and Production: *Lisa Hochstein*

Library of Congress Cataloging-in-Publication Data

Peters, Craig, 1958-
  Steve Case : Internet genius of America Online / by Craig Peters.
      p. cm. — (Internet biographies)
Summary: A biography of businessman who started America Online, an Internet service provider, that merged with the largest entertainment company, Time Warner, in 2000.
Includes bibliographical references and index.
  ISBN 0-7660-1971-3
  1. Case, Stephen McConnell—Juvenile literature. 2. Businessmen—United States—Biography—Juvenile literature. 3. America Online, Inc.—History—Juvenile literature. 4. AOL Time Warner—History—Juvenile literature. 5. Consolidation and merger of corporations—United States—Juvenile literature. 6. Internet service providers—United States—History—Juvenile literature. 7. Online information services industry—United States—History—Juvenile literature. [1. Case, Stephen McConnell. 2. Businesspeople. 3. America Online, Inc. 4. AOL Time Warner. 5. Internet service providers. 6. Online information services industry.] I. Title. II. Series.
HE7583.U6 P47 2003
338.7'61004678'092—dc21
                                    2002153380
Printed in the United States of America

10 9 8 7 6 5 4 3 2 1

To Our Readers:
We have done our best to make sure all Internet addresses in this book were active and appropriate when we went to press. However, the author and the publisher have no control over and assume no liability for the material available on those Internet sites or on other Web sites they may link to. Any comments or suggestions can be sent by e-mail to comments@enslow.com or to the address on the back cover.

Illustration Credits: America Online, p. 24; Associated Press/Wide World Photos, pp. 2, 9, 12, 15, 20, 29, 30, 32, 36; Corbis, p. 18; Reuters, p. 6.

Cover Illustration: Associated Press/Wide World Photos

Opposite Title Page: *From childhood paper routes to door-to-door sales, Steve Case has always been a businessman. He turned his passions for business and computers into a successful career as the head of America Online.*

CONTENTS

AOL chairman Steve Case, left, shakes hands with Time Warner chairman Gerald Levin as they seal a deal to combine their two companies, forming the largest media empire in the world.

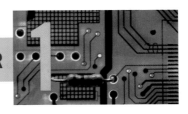

A Stunning Announcement

On January 10, 2000, an amazing handshake took place. One hand belonged to Gerald Levin. Levin was the chairman of the Time Warner Corporation. Time Warner was the largest entertainment company in the world, valued at $100 billion. How much is $100 billion? If you earned $10,000 a day, it would take you 27,400 years to earn $100 billion. Time Warner employed 70,000 people and owned cable channels like CNN, HBO, TBS, and the Cartoon Network. It owned popular magazines like *Time, People,* and *Sports Illustrated.* The Time Warner Corporation also owned the Warner Bros. television, movie, and music studios, and it created television hits like *ER* and *Friends.* Blockbuster movies created by Time Warner included *Harry Potter* and *Batman.* Recording artists under contract to Warner Bros. in 2000 included Madonna and Faith Hill.

Time Warner was an entertainment giant with few rivals. It was also a company with deep roots.

Time magazine was first published in 1923. Warner Bros. opened their movie studio in 1918. They released the first talking motion picture ever, *The Jazz Singer,* in 1927. The story of Time Warner is also the story of entertainment in the twentieth century.

The other palm in the amazing handshake belonged to Steve Case, the chairman of America Online (AOL). AOL was the largest Internet service provider (ISP) in the world. It provided Internet access to nearly 20 million people. AOL employed about 12,000 people. The company's worth was valued at $163 billion.

Unlike Time Warner, AOL was not a company with a long history. The beginnings of AOL stretched back only to 1985. That was the year Case and his

AOL'S STOCK VALUE

America Online was able to purchase Time Warner because AOL's stock was valued so highly. As the price of a stock goes up, so does the overall value of the company. That enables the company to buy other companies.

On March 19, 1992, one share of AOL stock was worth $11.50. Two years later, in August 1994, that same share of stock was worth $70.

On January 10, 2000, when AOL's merger with Time Warner was announced, the price of a share of stock of AOL was $73.68. With hundreds of millions of shares of AOL stock issued, the company had a lot of money to work with.

One of the companies that Time Warner brought to its deal with AOL was Time Inc., which owns dozens of popular magazines including Time, People, *and* Fortune. *Critics of the merger feared the new company, AOL Time Warner, would control too much of the nation's media.*

friend, Jim Kimsey, started the company that later became AOL. The company "went public" in 1992, which means the general public could buy shares of ownership in the company through the stock market.

Levin and Case shook hands on January 10, 2000, to seal a deal. AOL was buying Time Warner for $165 billion in AOL stock. It was the largest stock deal in the history of the United States.

When AOL and Time Warner announced that they would become one company, the world looked on in amazement. The significance of the deal could not be overstated. AOL was the new kid on the block.

It had built its strength on a still unproven new medium called the Internet. Now it was purchasing a powerful corporation with a long history.

"This merger will launch the next Internet revolution,"[1] Case said at the press conference announcing

WHAT IS A STOCK SPLIT?

When a stock "splits," the owner of the stock receives additional stock for every share he or she owns. Typically, stocks will split "two for one," which means that for every share owned, the stockholder receives one additional share.

When stock splits occur, though, the value of the stock changes so that the total value of what the stockholder owns stays the same. For example, one share of stock valued at $50 that splits two for one becomes two shares of stock valued at $25 dollars each. The total value before and after the split, though, remains $50.

Why do companies split stock? Often, they hope that the lower price per share will mean more people will buy the stock, ensuring continued growth of the company.

That was certainly the case with AOL. Between the time the company went public in 1992 and the time it announced its merger with Time Warner in 2000, AOL stock split two for one seven times. That means that one share of stock owned in 1992 became 128 shares of stock by 2000. As a result, $11.50 invested in one share of AOL in 1992 was worth $9,431.04 (a price of $73.68 per share multiplied by 128 shares) by the time of the AOL Time Warner merger announcement in 2000.

the deal. The merger would allow AOL Time Warner to tap into the full potential of the Internet. They could offer new services that would enrich people's lives. Case wanted to make the Internet an even more important part of everyday life.[2]

Before the merger could be completed, the deal had to be approved by the Federal Communications Commission (FCC). Their job was to make sure the new company wasn't so big and powerful that it became a monopoly, which was illegal in the United States. In a monopoly, only one company has control over a product or a service. When that happens, there is no competition in the marketplace. The company with the monopoly can raise its prices to customers who have nowhere else to go for the product. That, of course, is bad news for customers.

If the merger were approved, Case would become the chairman of the board of the new company, AOL Time Warner, valued at $350 billion.

Steve Case's company, AOL, had defined the Internet for over 20 million subscribers. Now he could define the Internet for a much larger audience. He would be leading the largest entertainment company in the world.

Steve Case was born and raised in Hawaii, home to natural wonders like this multi-level waterfall on the Kohala coast.

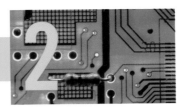

A Born Businessman

Stephen McDonnell Case was born August 21, 1958, in Honolulu, Hawaii. His father, Dan, was a corporate lawyer. His mother, Carol, was a schoolteacher. Both of Steve's parents were born and raised in Hawaii.

Steve grew up on the island of Oahu in Hawaii. The third of four children, he had an older brother, Daniel Case III, an older sister, Carin, and a younger brother, Jeff.

Born just thirteen months apart, Steve and his brother Dan were especially close. From an early age, they began looking for business opportunities. When Steve was just six years old, he and Dan sold limeade from a roadside stand. They charged two cents a cup. The limes came from their backyard. A few years later, the brothers formed Case Enterprises. They sold greeting cards and seeds door to door and by mail. "We made a fortune," Dan told *Business Week* magazine in 1996, "tens of dollars."[1]

The brothers also sold ad circulars and shared a newspaper route, rising early to deliver papers to their neighbors. They even became the Hawaiian distributor for a Swiss watchmaker, but they didn't sell one watch.

Like most teenagers, Steve enjoyed music, and he wrote album reviews for the school newspaper. He enjoyed basketball and bodysurfing. He was also a good student. His brother Dan described him as "normal, relatively shy, and creative."[2]

After graduating from high school, Steve went to Williams College in Massachusetts. He majored in political science, because, he told *Business Week,* "it was the closest thing to marketing."[3] As a student, "he was quiet, but thoughtful," said Professor Mark Taylor.[4] In his spare time, Steve served as a lead singer for two musical groups.

After graduating from Williams College in 1980, Case went to work for the Procter & Gamble Company as a junior brand manager. For two years he worked in the hair products division.

In 1982, Case left Procter & Gamble and joined the Pizza Hut division of PepsiCo. As manager of new pizza development, he was always traveling. During the day, he visited Pizza Hut restaurants across the country. He sampled new kinds of pizza and developed ideas for toppings. At night, he was developing a fascination for a new technology: the personal computer.

The portable computer that Steve Case carried while on the road for Pizza Hut was called a Kaypro. It was quite different from today's slim, lightweight laptops. The Kaypro computers of the early 1980s were hefty boxes. A Kaypro 10 model measured eighteen inches wide, nine inches high, and seventeen inches deep. It had a small nine-inch monitor that displayed twenty-four lines of text. The machine weighed twenty-six pounds. Though it sounds bulky by today's standards, it was considered a portable computer at that time.

Some of the earliest portable computers, on the middle shelf at left, weighed thirty pounds or more. Steve Case took a twenty-six pound Kaypro portable computer with him on business trips in the early 1980s.

For storage space, the Kaypro 10 had a ten megabyte hard drive. (A megabyte is a measure of how much information a computer can store.) Ten megabytes of information fills up seven floppy disks. The Kaypro 10 had a tiny fraction of the average hard drive space on a computer today. Its modem speed was slow. Yet the Kaypro 10 was a state-of-the-art system in 1982. It cost approximately $1,595, more than what a faster, more powerful laptop computer costs today.

While working for Pizza Hut, Case was a member of The Source, an early online community. At night, Case used his Kaypro to log on to The Source from his hotel room. He spent hours chatting with other members. He liked to read the messages posted on

THE SOURCE OF CASE'S ONLINE PASSION

The Source was an early online service. It was created in 1979 and based in McLean, Virginia. At its peak in 1989, The Source had 53,000 users. The Source offered news services, shopping and games, an online encyclopedia, and an airline reservation service, among other things.

Reader's Digest bought a majority interest in the company in 1980, but sold it in 1987. The tax preparation giant H&R Block purchased The Source in 1989. It shut it down less than two months later. Subscribers to The Source were merged with those of another online service, CompuServe, which was also owned by H&R Block.

online bulletin boards. "I thought there was something magic in sitting in a hotel room and connecting to all of this," Case said.[5]

Steve Case had envisioned the future. One day millions of other people would feel as excited as he did about the Internet and the ability to interact online. But he still had a long way to go before he would capture that magic with a company called America Online.

In 1983, Steve Case went to work for Control Video, a company that adapted popular Atari video games like these to personal computers.

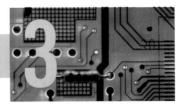

The Birth of AOL

I n 1983, Steve Case was getting restless. His work experiences at Procter & Gamble and Pizza Hut had not been fulfilling. Case later described these jobs as disasters. He said, "Managing a mature business is not my thing."[1]

But opportunity soon knocked for Case. In 1983, he and his brother Dan attended an electronics show in Las Vegas. At the show, Dan introduced Steve to the founders of the Control Video Corporation. Control Video provided downloadable Atari video games for personal computers. The company was struggling, but it offered Steve a job as a marketing assistant. He accepted on the spot.

"Job-hoppers don't wind up anywhere," Steve's father said. He thought Steve should not have left Pizza Hut. He told Steve, "this new job seems a little crazy."[2]

It did seem crazy. Control Video Corporation was in trouble and owed a lot of money. Financial

While working for Control Video, Steve Case helped develop online services for the Commodore, left, one of the first popular personal computers.

problems forced the company's board of directors to fire the management team. Among the few employees left in the company were Jim Kimsey, Marc Seriff, and Steve Case. Kimsey handled the company's financial affairs. Seriff was in charge of technology. Steve Case marketed the company's products.

After two years of struggling, Control Video made a deal with the Commodore Computer company. At that time, Commodore was the leading maker of personal computers. Commodore wanted to create an online service for users of its Commodore 64 computer. Control Video got the job.

Case helped chief executive officer (CEO) Jim Kimsey raise money to keep their company going, and Control Video renamed itself Quantum

Computer Services. It launched the Q-Link online service in 1985. It was hardly a service to brag about. Q-Link was only available on weeknights and weekends. Even so, Case and Quantum forged ahead. They managed to sign deals with two more computer makers. By 1987, Case had worked out a deal to provide online service to two popular brands of personal computers: Apple and Tandy. Q-Link offered AppleLink for users of Apple computers, and PC-Link for users of Tandy computers.

Quantum was spending a lot of money, though. Some of its associates thought Case was the wrong man for the job. "I had most of my venture-capital board members calling for him to be fired," Kimsey recalled later.[3] Kimsey liked Case, though, and was training him to one day be his replacement as CEO.

WHAT IS VENTURE CAPITAL?

Few companies start off with a lot of money in the bank and a line of customers waiting for the company's product. It takes money to start a new company, find customers, and get to the point where the company is making a profit.

That's where venture capital comes in. Venture capital is money that is invested in a company in exchange for partial ownership of that company. The person providing the money is called a venture capitalist. Venture capitalists gamble that the company will grow and become successful. Then they will make more money from their investment.

The two men had invested a lot of money and time in the company. They were the decision-makers at Quantum. They were working hard toward creating strong futures for the company and themselves.

Growth wasn't happening fast enough for many of the people involved with Quantum, however. In 1989, the combined membership of the Q-Link, AppleLink, and PC-Link services was only 75,000 users. Apple wanted to get out of its deal with Quantum in order to start its own online service. It offered Quantum $2.5 million to break their deal. Quantum took the money.

After its association with Apple came to an end, Quantum combined its online services under one

ONLINE SERVICES IN THE EARLY 1990s

In 1992 several companies saw the potential of providing online services to computer users. Most people had heard of companies like CompuServe and Prodigy. America Online, however, ranked a distant fourth among online services. Yet, in 1992, it was adding new members at the rate of approximately 145 per day.

COMPANY	MEMBERSHIP IN 1992
CompuServe	1,500,000
Prodigy	1,000,000
GEnie	350,000
America Online	155,000

brand name with a new image. In 1991, a company-wide contest was held to come up with a new name. Some of the suggestions included "Quantum 2000," "Explore," "Infinity," and Case's own suggestion, "Online America." The words in Case's suggestion were flip-flopped, and America Online was born.

America Online worked hard to become known as a user-friendly online service. As a result, its popularity grew. Another company, CompuServe, tried to buy the company for $50 million in 1991, but Case and Kimsey refused to sell.

In 1992, Case took over as CEO of America Online. As CEO, Case was responsible for everything AOL did. Under his leadership, America Online became a public company. The sale of AOL stock raised $66 million. This money was used to help the company grow. At the time, AOL had 250 employees and 155,000 subscribers. Both of those numbers were about to increase rapidly.

To attract new customers, America Online gives away CDs offering a free trial of AOL software.

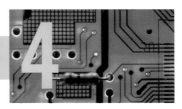

Spectacular Growth

After America Online went public, Steve Case led the company on a massive membership drive. AOL software disks began appearing everywhere. The disks offered people a chance to try AOL for free. They seemed to appear in every mailbox in every town in every state. They were attached to music CDs and boxes of cereal. They were inserted into magazines. They were handed out with Blockbuster video rentals. They were given out with meals on United Airlines flights.

AOL worked hard to reach potential customers. It also expanded its content offerings—the information featured on its service. After all, if the company was going to ask users to pay $2.95 per hour for AOL, then it needed to provide something for them to do. AOL made deals with hundreds of companies. They agreed to provide different entertainment and information for AOL users. Organizing all of this content was difficult. Case wanted to make AOL as easy as possible for customers to use. He wanted them to be comfortable using AOL to navigate on the Internet.

Content on AOL was divided into "channels" to help customers find what they were looking for. There was an Entertainment Channel. It included information and games about movies, television, and music. The Sports Channel provided the latest scores. It also had information about football, baseball, basketball, hockey, golf, auto racing, and even cricket, a popular English sport. The Kids Only Channel had special games and activities for young people. There were many other channels. AOL also offered news and weather reports, message boards, and chat rooms. There was just about any kind of information anyone could want. It was all presented in a user-friendly format.

In the mid-1990s, the Internet was still new to most Americans. Sports fans, for example, were not used to being able to get the latest sports scores, schedules, and news online. They were not used to reading comments about the teams and games from other sports fans. The fact that they could now talk to those fans in real time in a chat room was downright amazing.

That's the sort of impact Case wanted to have in all Americans' lives, and that was the impact AOL was having. When people received an AOL disk in the mail, they were likely to use the free trial. When they did, they discovered a brand-new way of communicating. This new mode of communication caught on quickly.

Sports fans were connecting with other sports fans via message boards. Movie fans were chatting with each other about their favorite stars and films. Americans were learning how to use e-mail—text messages that with just one click could be sent to another person's computer across the street, across the country, or around the world. Everyone wanted to experience what it was like to chat with someone, using a computer.

Under Case's direction, AOL membership grew from 155,000 in 1992 to 4 million in 1995. Using e-mail became almost as common for many Americans as using conventional mail, the telephone, or any other form of communication.

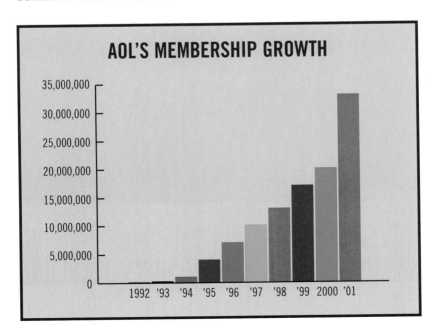

In 1996, AOL changed the way it charged for its service. Instead of charging by the hour, AOL decided to charge a flat fee. For $19.95 a month, customers could have unlimited access to AOL. Membership continued to soar, reaching 10 million in 1997.

Through it all, Case, whose friends describe him as a "workaholic," had to perform a balancing act. When AOL switched to flat-rate pricing, members began using the service more than ever. This placed enormous burdens on AOL's computer network. It meant that some people experienced repeated busy signals when they tried to dial into the service.

WHY CONSUMERS LOVED FLAT-RATE PRICING

In 1996, AOL switched from charging by the hour to charging by the month for its services. From the chart below, it's easy to see why customers welcomed the change. It's also easy to see how the change resulted in AOL's computer systems being overloaded by usage. Even a customer who spent an average of one hour a day online saw a savings of $68.55 per month.

TIME SPENT ONLINE IN A MONTH	1995 AOL COST	1996 AOL COST
one hour	$ 2.95	$19.95
five hours	$ 14.75	$19.95
ten hours	$ 29.50	$19.95
twenty hours	$ 59.00	$19.95
thirty hours	$ 88.50	$19.95
fifty hours	$147.50	$19.95

As CEO of America Online, Steve Case was always looking for ways to make AOL user-friendly. AOL gave away free software and charged users a flat fee for unlimited access. It also invested millions in network infrastructure to bring its services to customers faster.

This frustrated some customers. Case responded by investing $285 million in new computers and cables that could carry AOL services to customers faster. He saw customer complaints as a positive sign for the company.

"The level of passion that people felt about not being able to connect to AOL . . . was somewhat staggering," Case told the *Washington Post* in 1998,

> considering it was only a few years ago [that] I had trouble explaining even to my parents what I was doing. If AOL five years ago had been inaccessible for a weekend, nobody would have known or cared. We

were like a little hobby people played with. Suddenly, now we were more part of the everyday life. If we weren't there, there were big problems.[1]

This was a time of great change in Case's personal life, too. In 1996, he and his wife Joanne, whom he had met in college, separated. They had been married for eleven years and had three children.

In 1997, AOL purchased its former rival, CompuServe, which had only 2.6 million subscribers. One year later, in July 1998, Case married Jean Villenueva, a former Vice President of Corporate Communications for AOL.

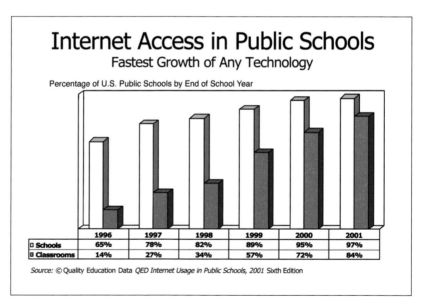

Internet Access in Public Schools
Fastest Growth of Any Technology

Percentage of U.S. Public Schools by End of School Year

	1996	1997	1998	1999	2000	2001
Schools	65%	78%	82%	89%	95%	97%
Classrooms	14%	27%	34%	57%	72%	84%

Source: © Quality Education Data *QED Internet Usage in Public Schools, 2001* Sixth Edition

In the late 1990s, Internet use increased dramatically. This graph shows how quickly public schools began using the Internet as a tool for learning. By the end of the 2001–2002 school year, 97 percent of public schools offered Internet access to students.

As the 1990s drew to a close, people all over the world rushed to get connected to this incredible new thing called the Internet. AOL firmly established itself as the leading online service among consumers. Leadership and success in the online industry, however, was only a hint of things to come for AOL and Steve Case.

Steve Case's mission in life is to make sure the Internet impacts society in positive ways. He spoke at the Internet conference "Focus on the Children," which explored ways to make the Internet safer for kids.

CHAPTER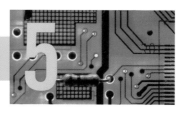

AOL: The Future of the Internet?

The merger of America Online with Time Warner was announced on January 10, 2000. One year later, the Federal Communications Commission approved the merger. A new company, AOL Time Warner, was born.

Steve Case believed the Internet and AOL Time Warner could bring a brighter future to the world. AOL had nearly 30 million users by the middle of 2001. It accounted for nearly one-third of all the time spent online in the United States in 2001.[1]

Now it had the ability to tap into Time Warner's vast news and entertainment reserves. The news gathering abilities of the CNN network, for example, could be combined with the information-spreading ability of AOL.

AOL Time Warner was a media giant. Nobody knew quite where the company was headed, or what it thought it could accomplish. Advances in home computing and Internet access had been rapid in the

1990s. The first decade of the twenty-first century was poised to bring more radical changes.

Case wanted to provide the happiest possible experience for his customers. As a result, privacy and security became two very important issues for AOL. People who sign up for the service don't want their personal information, such as address and credit card numbers, given to any other companies. They don't want their e-mail to be read by anyone other than the person who is supposed to receive it. AOL developed a detailed privacy policy designed to protect the personal information of all its members.

AOL TIME WARNER: MORE THAN ONE COMPANY

To understand how big AOL Time Warner is, look at it as not just one company, but a collection of six businesses under one corporate umbrella.

BUSINESS	COMPANY
Interactive Services	America Online
Networks	Turner Broadcasting, Home Box Office
Publishing	Time Inc., Time Warner Trade Publishing
Filmed Entertainment	Warner Bros., New Line Cinema
Music	Warner Music Group
Cable Systems	Time Warner Cable

Case, a father himself, made sure AOL protected the safety of kids online. Parents don't want their children talking to strangers online, or exchanging e-mail with anyone they shouldn't. Letting a child explore the online world alone is like letting a child explore a big city alone. AOL responded to online safety concerns by developing special content areas for kids, and by providing parents with tools to limit their child's activities on the Internet.

Case was also committed to linking people with opportunities via the Internet. Under his direction, AOL was brought into classrooms. The AOL@School online learning system was designed to enhance student learning from grades K to 12. To connect citizens with elected officials, AOL launched its Government Guide. At Case's request, AOL launched Helping.org, an online means of charitable giving.

"The future is much more than just bytes and bandwidth, Web sites or streaming videos," Case said. He envisioned a future in which the Internet continued to affect people's lives in new ways. "We can build bridges between devices," he said, ". . . and make the first Internet revolution quaint by comparison."[2]

Steve Case poses with actress Julia Roberts, left, at a movie premiere in 2001. As CEO of AOL Time Warner, Case represented the company at public events. AOL Time Warner owns the Warner Bros. movie studio.

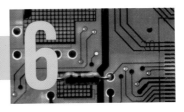

Epilogue

Steve Case has traveled a remarkable path. As a boy, he sold limeade for two cents a cup. As an adult, he headed the largest entertainment and communications company in the world.

As the twenty-first century began, Case withdrew from the day-to-day operations of American Online. There used to be a monthly letter from Case on AOL. That ended with the AOL Time Warner merger. As chairman of AOL Time Warner, Case represents the company at business conferences and major public events.

Much of Case's time, though, is spent on charitable endeavors through the Case Foundation, which he founded with his wife Jean. The Case Foundation funds programs that help to expand digital opportunities for young people in inner cities and rural areas. Case also spends a lot of time with his family. In December 2000, he bought 22,000 acres of land, mostly farms, in Kauai, Hawaii. In 2001, *Forbes*, a leading business magazine, ranked him as the 211th richest American. He is worth an estimated $1.1 billion.

Of course, he does keep in touch with AOL management. In 2001, he told *Fortune* magazine that management gives him "a sense of what's happening and [a chance to] provide my perspective where appropriate, without running the risk of meddling too much in the day to day."[1]

AOL Time Warner faced hard times in 2002, when the company's stock price dropped to its lowest point since the merger. AOL's membership growth also slowed. Critics speculated that perhaps the merger of AOL and Time Warner would not be as successful as predicted.

At the same time, Steve Case endured personal hardship with the loss of his older brother Dan, who died of cancer in June of 2002. Despite these difficulties, Steve Case remained chairman of AOL Time Warner, and he continued to work hard to make the company as successful as it could be.

Case, like each of us, lives in a remarkable age. The Internet has been an agent of tremendous change. It took decades for radio and television to be welcomed into American households. By contrast, the Internet became a part of our everyday lives in just a few years.

The Internet has changed the way we work, play, and live. Yet the Internet's influence is only starting to be understood. There are still many unanswered questions about the Internet. How will it affect our lives now that millions of citizens can share ideas with the click of a mouse? How will children who grow up with the Internet be different than their parents?

"Our vision has been the same for a decade," Case told *Business Week*. "We're building a new medium with a transforming impact on people's lives, and on society, and the economy. We've positioned AOL at the epicenter of that revolution."[2]

AOL was at the center of a revolution in the way society used all kinds of information. If information is power, then the Internet was creating the most powerful generation the world had ever known. With AOL delivering more than half the nation's online access, the most powerful generation can thank Steve Case for its strength.

CHRONOLOGY

1958 Stephen McDonnell Case is born in Honolulu, Hawaii, on August 21.

1980 Case graduates from Williams College and goes to work for Procter & Gamble.

1982 Case becomes a manager for Pizza Hut; while on the road, he frequents an online community called The Source.

1983 Case accepts a job as a marketing assistant with Control Video Corporation.

1985 Quantum Computer Services, formerly Control Video, launches the Q-Link Online service; Case marries his first wife, Joanne.

1991 Quantum Computer Services renames itself America Online.

1992 Case takes over as CEO of America Online; the online service has approximately 155,000 members; America Online becomes a public company on March 19.

1996 America Online begins charging a flat fee for its online service; Case separates from his first wife, Joanne.

1997 America Online purchases its rival, CompuServe.

1998 Case marries his second wife, Jean.

2000 The proposed merger between America Online and Time Warner is announced on January 10; the FCC begins its review of the merger on March 27.

2001 America Online accounts for approximately one-third of all time spent online in the United States; the merger between America Online and Time Warner is approved by the FCC on January 11; Steve Case becomes chairman of the board of AOL Time Warner, Inc.; Steve Case's net worth is estimated at $1.1 billion.

2002 Worldwide AOL membership surpasses 34 million.

CHAPTER NOTES

CHAPTER ONE. A Stunning Announcement

1. *AOL-Time Warner Merger,* Online NewsHour, January 10, 2000, <http://www.pbs.org/newshour/bb/business/jan-june00/aol_01-10a.html> (March 20, 2002).

2. Ibid.

CHAPTER TWO. A Born Businessman

1. Amy Cortese, Amy Barrett, Paul Eng, and Linda Himelstein, "The Online World of Steve Case," *Business Week,* April 15, 1996, pp. 78-83.

2. Ibid.

3. Ibid.

4. "A Steve Case Study," *ABCNews.com,* 2000, http://204.202.137.112/ sections/business/DailyNews/case990110.html> (March 20, 2002).

5. Cortese et al., pp. 78-83.

CHAPTER THREE. The Birth of AOL

1. Amy Cortese, Amy Barrett, Paul Eng, and Linda Himelstein, "The Online World of Steve Case," *Business Week,* April 15, 1996, pp. 78-83.

2. "Steve Case: Career @ A Glance", *Career Magazine,* February 29, 2000, <http://qa.justpeople.com/ContentNew/People/Leaders/leaderdb/SteveCase. asp> (March 20, 2002).

3. Cortese et al., pp. 78-83.

CHAPTER FOUR. Spectacular Growth

1. "A Conversation with Stephen M. Case," *The Washington Post.com,* 1998, <http://www.washingtonpost.com/wp-srv/business/longterm/conversation /case/case.htm> (March 20, 2002).

CHAPTER FIVE. AOL: The Future of the Internet

1. "AOL-TW: The Present Looks Great, but What of the Future?" *Internet.com,* February 27, 2001, <http://cyberatlas.internet.com/big_picture/ traffic_patterns/article /0,,5931_599991,00.html> (March 20, 2002).

2. Wylie Wong and Troy Wolverton, "Case Equates 'AOL Anywhere' with Net's Future," *CNet News.com,* April 5, 2000, <http://news.cnet.com/news /0-1005-200-1644745.html> (March 20, 2002).

CHAPTER SIX. Epilogue

1. Marc Gunther, "Where's Steve?" *Fortune,* July 23, 2001, p. 92.

2. "At the Epicenter of the Revolution," *Business Week.com,* September 16, 1999, <http://www.businessweek.com:/ebiz/9909/916case.htm> (March 20, 2002).

GLOSSARY

bandwidth—The amount of information that can be carried by the wires and cables that connect a user to the Internet.

baud—A measure of the speed of a computer modem. The baud rate measures the number of times per second a modem signal changes. Early modems communicated at 300 baud, transferring information at 300 bits per second. A 28.8 modem operates at 2,400 baud, with each signal change communicating 12 bits of information.

bytes—The building blocks of computer information, expressed as ones and zeros. One byte is composed of eight bits (a single zero or one).

CEO—Chief Executive Officer, the person in a company who is responsible for the overall activities of that company.

e-mail—Electronic mail, a way of sending messages from one computer user to another.

entrepreneur—One who organizes, manages, and assumes the risks of a business enterprise.

Federal Communications Commission (FCC)—The U.S. government agency charged with regulating interstate and international communications by radio, television, wire, satellite, and cable.

hyperlink—An easy way of accessing one Web site document from another Web site document. Hyperlinks are most often presented as underlined blue text.

Internet—The system of worldwide connected computer networks, of which the World Wide Web is a part.

Internet Service Provider (ISP)—A company that offers customers access to the Internet, usually for a monthly fee.

megabyte—A measure of information storage, equivalent to 1,048,576 bytes.

modem—The device that enables a computer to communicate with other computers over telephone lines.

stock market—A financial exchange where orders to buy and sell stocks are brought together and filled by brokers acting as agents for the public.

URL—Uniform Resource Locator, the address of any given page on the Internet. A complete URL, for example, would be: http://www.aol.com.

venture capital—Money invested in small, young companies in return for partial ownership of the company with the hope of rapid company growth.

Web site—A location on the World Wide Web. Many Web sites are constantly changing and evolving, and may include sound and video along with graphics and information.

World Wide Web—A hypertext-based Internet service that organizes information using a wide variety of linked documents.

FURTHER READING

Kaufield, John, and Steve Case. *America Online for Dummies.* New York: Hungry Minds, Inc., 1999.

Stauffer, David M. *Business the AOL Way: Secrets of the World's Number 1 WebMaster.* Dover, New Hampshire: Capstone Publishing, 2000.

Swisher, Karen. *AOL.COM: How Steve Case Beat Bill Gates, Nailed the Netheads, and Made Millions in the War for the Web.* New York: Times Books, 1998.

Thornally, George. *AOL BY GEORGE: The Inside Story of America Online.* Livingston, New Jersey: Urly Media, 1999.

Wooten, Terry. Planet *AOL: From "Anywhere" to "Everywhere" with Time Warner and Beyond.* Upper Saddle River, New Jersey: Prentice Hall, 2001.

INTERNET ADDRESSES

The official Web site of AOL Time Warner.
http://www.aoltimewarner.com

Steve Case's biography, posted on the official company Web site of AOL Time Warner.
http://www.aoltimewarner.com/corporate_information/bio/CaseSteph.adp

A March 3, 2000, interview with Steve Case, conducted by *Business Week* magazine.
http://www.businessweek.com:/2000/00_13/b3674020.htm

A timeline of events leading up to the FCC's January 11, 2000, approval of the AOL Time Warner merger.
http://www.usatoday.com/life/cyber/invest/ina516a.htm

INDEX